Roping the Storms of Life Like a Cowgirl

*A Creative Approach to
Finding Your Inner Strength and Confidence*

JAN PFLAUM

Copyright © 2020 Jan Pflaum

All rights reserved.

No part of this book may be reproduced in any form or by any electronic or mechanical means including information storage and retrieval systems without permission in writing from the author, except by a reviewer, who may quote brief passages in a review.

ISBN: 978-1-60414-986-9 (soft cover)

Photo of Jan by photographer Marla Sarokhanian
Location: Grapevine Consignment Market, Grapevine, Texas

Fideli Publishing, Inc.
119 W Morgan St.
Martinsville, IN 46151
888-343-3542
www.FideliPublishing.com

PRINTED IN THE UNITED STATES OF AMERICA

Cowgirls Have the Capability of Looking at Life Through the Lenses of Only the Possible!

Dedication

This book is dedicated to the cowgirls past and present that have exemplified their hard work, courage without fear and the never-ending possibilities of the journey that lay ahead of them.

Cowgirls have proven over and over again about trusting their instincts, taking risks and just enjoying the life that God gave them, through love and joy.

Table of Contents

	The Beginning...	xi
Chapter 1:	She Ropes a 1,000 Pound Steer... No Problem	1
Chapter 2:	A Cowgirl Believes a Bad Day is Not a Bad Life	7
Chapter 3:	The Spirit of a Cowgirl	13
Chapter 4:	The No Fear Factor of a Cowgirl	17
Chapter 5:	Circling the Barrel	23
Chapter 6:	A Cowgirl Moves Her Body with Music in Her Soul	29
Chapter 7:	The Trail Ahead	37
	Cowgirl Prayer	45

The Beginning...

The High Desert Princess, National Cowgirl Museum, Ft. Worth Texas.

From the Author

Moving to Texas and exploring the cowgirl mentality helped me to create this inspirational book.

Roping the Storms of Life Like a Cowgirl is designed to take you on a journey where you can tap into that cowgirl mentality. This mentality will give you the motivation to change your life so that you can leave behind being anxious, worried and fearful, and find a mindset of manifesting and capturing the courage you have inside of you. Cowgirls are strong, not by chance but because of the storms they go through and survive.

Cowgirls have given me not only a mission but a purpose and I'm writing through their inspiration and hope to reach out to those who are experiencing the absolute worst storms of their lives.

I am very thankful for the National Cowgirl Museum in Ft. Worth, Texas for giving me insight on these women, these cowgirls who have exemplified a zest for life, courage and, above all, the mentality that nothing, absolutely nothing is impossible.

With gratitude and love,
Jan Pflaum

Lucille Mulhall
1885-1940

Lucille was the best-known Western performer of her era, and was identified as a "cowgirl" before the term was widely used.

Competing with, and frequently beating, male competitors in steer roping events, Lucille helped make women an integral part of rodeo.

She was inducted into The National Rodeo Hall of Fame as America's first Cowgirl!

CHAPTER 1

She Ropes a 1,000-Pound Steer... No Problem

How is that cowgirl's down through the ages have been so courageous? How have they managed ranches, raised children, weathered the storms, dealt with losing animals, competed in rodeo's and the list goes on and on.

How have they done this?

They do it by not backing down from anything or anyone. They are manifested with true grit, determination, and a no fear factor.

You may say to yourself, "I don't live on a ranch, I am not out gathering cattle in the winter storms."

That might be true but...

You can certainly carry the cowgirl mentality inside of you to help you mentally weather your storm — the storm you are going through at this very moment.

I am really worried, scared,
and I feel alone in my struggles...

When these types of feelings try to overpower you, remember that God created cowgirls to show the rest of us how to be women who are fearless and courageous.

At this very moment you might be struggling with many issues in your life. You might have so many problems that it seems like they're totally overwhelming and impossible to resolve.

Let's back up and adjust our mentality a bit.

You are circling the barrel ... perhaps it's an illness, or a loss, a disability, a tragedy, or any number of other things that are getting you down in life. This is a time of experiencing steep slopes, exhausting trails, rocky terrain, but when you are a cowgirl, this is what you do:

You ride that Bronco — hang on, don't let go, and don't give up. Be persistent and ride it out. When the ride is over and you've made it through the tough times, lay down in the grass, look up and thank God for your life.

You may not be having a whooping good time but you are still here and you're still breathing. Praise Him.

Put on that cowgirl hat of yours and look ahead. Put on your boots and walk like you have a purpose.

Now you're ready to saddle up and rope that 1000-pound steer that keeps trying to disrupt your life. He thinks you don't have enough cowgirl power in you to get it done. He thinks he is in control. But there is one thing that this steer does not know — he is messing with the wrong cowgirl.

You are not going to allow that steer or anything else to get in your way. *You* have the ultimate power, and *you are the only one who has control of your life.*

It's true that what you do with your life is entirely up to you. You can choose to waste it or you can change your mindset with the help of the power of prayer. While your life may not be the life you imagined, you're still here and you have a journey to make. God has bestowed this life upon you, so you need to make up your mind to make it the best it can be.

You have just three choices in life:

Give Up

Give In

Or give it all you got.

Cowgirl, the choice is all up to you.

**CHAPTER 1
COWGIRL WORKSHEET**

Finding your Inner Cowgirl

Circle what applies to you.

1. Do you operate out of fear?
   Yes No

2. Do you want to change from living a life of fear to a life of strength?
   Yes No

3. If you decide to change... What do you need to do?

   (Circle what applies to you and add any other needs you want fulfilled after this list.)

Support	Be more open-minded
A positive attitude	Be more relaxed
Courage	_____
Faith	_____
Take better care of myself	_____

For God gave us a spirit not of fear but of power and love and self-control.

— 2 Timothy 1:7 ESV

I can do all things through him who strengthens me.

— Philippians 4:13 ESV

Do not be conformed to this world, but be transformed by the renewal of your mind, that by testing you may discern what is the will of God, what is good and acceptable and perfect.

— Romans 12:2 ESV

CHAPTER 2

Cowgirls Know a Bad Day Does Not Mean a Bad Life

The daily mindset of a cowgirl is fierce. She wakes up and starts her day with gratitude and thankfulness. She starts by thanking God for another day and another opportunity to begin again. She does not know where each day will take her, but she knows that perhaps her day might be filled with challenges.

Bring it on...

When life lasso's us with difficulties, it just seems as though it we'll never get free and be saddled with the struggles forever. Negative thinking can lead you to believe your life is just too hard, the pain is too intense, you'll never be healthy again, or you'll never get past the loss or the tragedy. The

struggle to get out of bed each morning might seem like more than you can bear. You just want to sleep and hope everything will be better when you wake up.

This does not have to be your life.

Socrates states: "The secret of change is to focus your energy, not on the old but on building the new."

There is a story about a wise cowgirl who was talking to a little boy. She told him, "There are two wolves always fighting inside of me. One is filled with anger, fear, regret, lies and shame. The other is filled with love, joy, forgiveness, truth and peace. This isn't true just for me, these wolves rage inside all of us."

The little boy thought for a moment and asked, "Which wolf will win?"

The wise cowgirl answered, "The one you feed."

Learn this wise cowgirl's lesson. Get up, feed yourself with prayerful gratitude and see how your life changes. You'll suddenly have the courage to turn your horse around in the right direction, and head toward the sunrise of your life.

A cowgirl stands tall and looks up to the heavens, crying out to God. She did this not because she was sad, but because she had to change. There were no other options for her.

**CHAPTER 2
COWGIRL WORKSHEET**

Roping the trails to my Success

What are you changing in order to rope your fears?

_____

_____

Are you being successful with your roping efforts?

_____

_____

What do you need to strengthen to do better?

_____

_____

I can do all things through him who strengthens me.
— Philippians 4:13

Be strong and courageous. Do not fear or be in dread of them, for it is the Lord your God who goes with you. He will not leave you or forsake you.
— Deuteronomy 31:6

CHAPTER 3

The Spirit of a Cowgirl

The saying above personifies cowgirl beliefs, and this is the way she lives. She looks at things with a broader perspective — not thinking about the negative but looking for the positive.

You can become that cowgirl with that unstoppable spirit if you take charge of your thoughts all day long. It is a fact that when you change the way you look at things, the things you look at change.

God tells us that He knew us before we were born and He wants our lives to overflow with love and purpose. Rope your storm with the mentality that you are not going to be defeated by any obstacle you are facing. You might not believe you have a purpose in this life, but oh, you do.

> *Your destiny is not to stay in this negative form of existence.*

You must stop the negative thinking. Don't go around thinking I am too sick to do this, I am too disabled to do that, or I am too old and have had too many tragedies to make changes. You must pull yourself out of this destructive mentality and plant the seed in your subconscious that you are worthy of moving on.

Take control of your thoughts and your life and begin to live for a purpose. Don't die with the music still in you. Get on your horse and ride into a place where you are giving joy to others. When you do that, you will find peace within you like you have never experienced before. Yours will become a positive journey.

When you change the way you look at things, you will begin to live in joy, and go around singing the music inside of you out loud and giving God's love away to others.

Cowgirls became a powerful feminine symbol, not because they weren't scared, but because they live strong and determined, despite their fears.

**CHAPTER 3
COWGIRL WORKSHEET**

Dropping the Reins of My Worthlessness

What thoughts do you need to change?
(Include all that apply and add your own.)

    I cannot win this battle.

    I don't deserve to win this battle.

    I am not a good fighter.

    No one really cares.

_____

_____

I am going to start exchanging my negative thoughts for positive ones.   Yes No

I am going to start helping others.   Yes No

Finally, be strong in the Lord and in the strength of his might.

—Ephesians 6:10

Miss Mamie Francis & Napoleon Date: ca. 1915-1922.

Courtesy of the National Cowgirl Museum and Hall of Fame, Ft. Worth Texas.

CHAPTER 4

The 'No Fear' Factor of a Cowgirl

Mamie Francis Hafley thrilled audiences with a horse diving act, riding off a fifty-foot-high platform into a barrel of water just ten feet across. She knew how to power herself with the "no fear" factor. Between 1908 and 1917 she performed the horse diving stunt a total of 628 times. This cowgirl had the ultimate "no fear" factor.

What does this tell you? She refused to occupy her mind with fear and worry because she had a mission.

Be a Mamie Francis Hafley, and realize that fear serves no purpose in your life. Soar above, and go beyond your fears.

Fear is:
False
Evidence
Appearing
Real

Fear does not come from God. He did not give us a spirit of fear.

Think about the issues you are facing at this very moment. How many of those issues are tied with fear? Do you honestly believe Mamie Francis Hafley, this amazing cowgirl, was afraid? I believe she could not have done her daredevil act 628 times if she was. Oh, she may have had a fleeting moment of fear, but did not let it interfere with her mission. She never let the fear of what *might* happen hold her back. This is the ultimate cowgirl spirit.

Cowgirls have done some of the most courageous stunts ever down through the years, and they are still doing them. So, you have no excuse not to soar above and go beyond your fears. This will be especially important during the times when you're facing adversities.

You may not jump into the water on a horse, but you certainly have what you need within you to enable you to take the leap into believing that you can soar above and beyond your fears and make it through the challenging times of your life.

So, cowgirl, get on that platform of yours, look straight at your goal and jump. Jump into that belief that you can conquer anything. You have that power within you — use it!

You'll find yourself looking at the rest of the world with a smile on your face and a victory wave as you shout, "I did it!"

Become the cowgirl that rides into the rodeo arena wearing a smile and a look of determination. Know without a doubt that you are going into this arena for the absolute ride of your life. Will you be scared? Absolutely! But you will find the courage to conquer the obstacles you face.

Look up and know you have three choices:

Give Up. Give In. Or Give it all you got!

Tell yourself:

> *"I am a winner.*
> *I only look at life through*
> *the lenses of the possible.*
> *I am that cowgirl!"*

Gain Release from Your Chute

Conquor Fear and Boundaries

What issues are you facing now that are causing you great fear?

_____
_____
_____

What fears will you face using your new Cowgirl mentality?

_____
_____
_____

What have you conquered?

_____
_____
_____

Who or what helped you conquer?
_____
_____
_____

Are you celebrating?   Yes   No
Why or Why not?

_____
_____
_____

Fear not, for I am with you; be not dismayed, for I am your God; I will strengthen you, I will help you, I will uphold you with my righteous right hand.

— Isaiah 41:10

CHAPTER 5

Circling the Barrel

You may be going through the journey of your life right at this very moment. It might be a journey you don't know you'll survive. You don't know what tomorrow will hold, you only know that today is bringing lots of pain and agony. Because you're in this bad place, perhaps you're thinking about failure, fear, and regrets, and like nothing is working for you.

Close your eyes. Take a deep breath. Exhale and release all the negative thinking that is crowding your thoughts. Know and believe that you are not fighting these battles on your own — God has His eye on you. By using the power of faith, you can move your mountains of anxiety onto a new positive trail.

How do you think cowgirls have survived down through the centuries? They survive with faith, and by having the mindset that they can conquer anything. When you find your inner Cowgirl, you will realize that you can also conquer anything you may be facing.

* * * *

I would like to relate a story of my friend Sarah, a brave cowgirl and barrel racer. She was an excellent competitor and very successful.

One day when she was competing in a rodeo she fell from her horse and injured her eye. The injury was so severe that she lost the vision in her right eye.

Sometime later I was talking with Sarah and she told me, "You know this accident was an extremely devastating blow to my life. I dearly treasured the sport and I had to make a difficult decision. I asked myself, do I stop competing in Barrell Racing or do I continue riding in the sport that I love? I decided that I could not allow this accident to stop me from doing something that brings me such joy. I have *not* ridden in my last rodeo."

Sarah kept saying and trusting that she was going to get back on her horse and be a champion again. It was not easy for her, but she did it.

She didn't surrender to her disability. She went on to compete, wearing a patch over her eye, but she never wore a patch over her spirit. She continued to be a successful barrel racer, a winner and a shining cowgirl.

Sarah told me several years later that God used her recovery and courage to help others who were also struggling with disabilities and personal issues. Her example encouraged others to keep fighting.

Do you want to possess that cowgirl mindset? You have the ultimate power within you to be a champion and gain victory over whatever obstacles you are facing. Nothing, cowgirl, nothing is going to hold you back from circling your barrel.

Just an added note that barrel racing is one of the most popular events in the rodeo, and it is where women shine. Somehow, that's not surprising!

CHAPTER 5
COWGIRL WORKSHEET

Cowgirl, You are Not a Victim

Do you feel you are you in a race for your life right now? Yes   No

Why?_____
_____

Are you successfully conquering your fears?
 Yes   No

How?_____
_____

Are you going to continue to fight your battles with a positive attitude? Yes   No

How?_____
_____

Describe what keeps your positive attitude going strong?

_____
_____

What are you doing to help others with the knowledge you've gained?

_____
_____

How are others helping you?

_____
_____

Be strong and courageous. Do not fear or be in dread of them, for it is the Lord your God who goes with you. He will not leave you or forsake you.

— Deuteronomy 31:6

But they who wait for the Lord shall renew their strength; they shall mount up with wings like eagles; they shall run and not be weary; they shall walk and not faint. — Isaiah 40:31

CHAPTER 6

A Cowgirl Moves Her Body with Music in Her Soul

Cowgirls were among the first professional athletes in the United States. Their magnitude of personal power was astonishing. Not only did they have the power within them to be winners, but they also knew how to take care of their bodies so they could achieve their goals.

Exercise is one of the key components of having a healthy mind, body and soul. When exercise becomes a habit, it makes you feel good because it releases the natural chemicals endorphins and serotonin, and they help to battle fatigue and improve your mood.

Whether you're facing an illness or going through other challenges in life, a daily exercise

routine will absolutely give you an energy boost throughout your day. Even if you are going through chemotherapy or radiation treatments, there are exercise programs specifically designed for you. Ask your physician or oncologist now, and ... get moving!

If you aren't involved in some sort of exercise program, you are going to be stuck in your unhealthy body. Exercise doesn't have to be extreme. Walking is one of the best forms of exercise there is. You can reap all the physical and mental health benefits of exercise with just a 30-minute walk every day. If you are not able to do the full 30 minutes at once, split it in half. You'll still reap the same benefits and be comfortable while you do it.

You might think exercising is going to sap your energy, but just the opposite is true. Exercise gives you more energy, reduces fatigue and perks up your mood.

Also remember that hydration while exercising and throughout the day is equally important to your overall health. Drink water and only water, before, during and after you exercise, and make it a habit to hydrate all during your day.

Exercise can be a great way to get some time to yourself. Put in your ear phones and listen to your favorite music while tuning out the rest of the world. Music is a powerful stimuli that touches your heart and soul like nothing else can.

Even cowgirls on the rodeo circuit use in music therapy to give them a boost of positive energy as they work to become champions.

If you haven't already incorporated exercise and music into your life, now is the time to create an action plan. Include some of the items below and come up with others of your own:

- Be prayerful with gratitude.
- Take a break during the day from social media.
- Switching off your computer and reboot yourself just like your computer.

- Go somewhere that is quiet and peaceful and read a book.
- Call a friend to chat, don't text.
- Play some favorite music that brings back happy memories.
- Plan ahead and take a day trip.
- Spoil yourself, have an ice cream cone or devour a hand full of M&Ms (or more)!

Making one or more of these adjustments in your daily life, along with your daily exercise routine will be so therapeutic you will want to put on some George Strait tunes and dance all around the house.

Life is full of disappointments, failures and setbacks, but none of those things can permanently stop you. You have the power to overcome anything that life throws at you. There is nothing as powerful as a made-up mind. No person, situation or circumstance can define who you are. God has an overflow victory designed just for you. Don't give up, cave in, or stop believing in yourself, Cowgirl. The ride is not over, and your music never stops.

You are a Winner!

Barrel Out of Your Defensive Mode

Are you exercising? Yes   No

Do you need to step-up your exercise program?

Yes   No

Which exercises do you plan to add to your routine?

_____

_____

_____

Do you listen to music while exercising?

Yes   No

How do you feel music helps you when exercisting?

_____

_____

_____

What is your daily plan of action to improve your attitude?

_____

_____

_____

What attitudes have you adopted into your life that have changed the way you think?

_____

_____

_____

Are these changes beneficial? Yes No

But he said to me, "My grace is sufficient for you, for my power is made perfect in weakness." Therefore, I will boast all the more gladly of my weaknesses, so that the power of Christ may rest upon me. For the sake of Christ, then, I am content with weaknesses, insults, hardships, persecutions, and calamities. For when I am weak, then I am strong. — 2 Corinthians 12:9-10

CHAPTER 7

The Trail Ahead

A cowgirl must gallop fast and work a big lasso to achieve her goals. She knows that when the riding gets tough, you tilt your hat down, use your spurs and get the job done. To quote Montana Cowgirl Mary McConnell Roberts, "Cowgirl is a broad term that blankets many people with a common thread, and that thread is the spirit."

You may not be a cowgirl, or raised cattle, ridden a horse, for that matter even worn a pair of cowgirl boots, but you do have challenges to face that require a Cowgirl Mentality. At times your life's journey may seem like a long and exhausting trail, and you might not be certain where it's taking you. When things get tough, ask yourself: "How am

I going to survive? How am I going to ride the trail ahead?"

If your answers to those questions are anything but positive, then stop. Your trail will be a rougher ride when you're carrying around a negative attitude. Take some time to evaluate your life and what you hope to accomplish, then create a plan for achieving your goals.

You might be thinking, "I have a terminal illness. There's nothing positive about my life." You're going down the wrong trail of thinking. You have the ability to choose to *not* ride that trail. Turn your horse around and find an uplifting path.

Every day when you wake up, tap into your Cowgirl Spirit before you start your day. Before ever getting out of bed, think about what you have already achieved with your Cowgirl Spirit, and why you should be grateful for all that you have accomplished on your journey.

Gratefulness transcends limitations. Let me say it again, *gratefulness transcends limitations.*

Recite this is prayer of gratitude each morning:

I know the trail ahead is going to be a challenge but I am not afraid. This is not going to destroy my life. I am a child of God and I have far too many trails to ride too many missions to accomplish and I am grateful for each day.

Focus on today. Let go of yesterday. Remind yourself every day: This is the only day I have and the only life I have, so I must live it to the fullest.

Don't allow your subconscious mind to feed your spirit with thoughts of fear, worry and anxiety. Believing those negative subconscious thoughts can cause you to feel totally lost. If you trust your subconscious mind, you are allowing the door to close to your Cowgirl Spirit. Instead, use your Cowgirl Spirit to chase away those thoughts and feelings and guide you to a more positive state of mind.

Put your Cowgirl Spirit into action. Rope that survivor mentality and look at illness, tragedy or loss head on and say, "You are *not* going to destroy my life, and you certainly are not going to stop me."

"She is clothed with strength and dignity and has no fear of the future." —Proverbs 31:25

Have powerful faith in yourself and in God and developing a Cowgirl Mentality will come easily. Now it's time to climb into your saddle and get ready for the ride that takes you to infinite possibilities.

And then it happens...

One day you wake up and you're in this place where everything feels right. Your heart is calm. Your soul is lit. Your thoughts are positive. Your vision is clear. You're at peace with what you have been through and at peace with where you are headed.

This cowgirl is ready for anything life throws at her. BRING IT ON!

CHAPTER 7
COWGIRL WORKSHEET

Creating My Cowgirl Life
Changing My Habits, Focus, Self-Worth

Have you been successful in creating your Cowgirl Spirit? Yes   No

Where will the trail you have chosen take you?

_____
_____
_____

What habits have you changed?

_____
_____
_____

What is your current focus?

_____
_____
_____

How have you strengthened your self-worth?

_____

_____

_____

Have I not commanded you? Be strong and courageous. Do not be frightened, and do not be dismayed, for the Lord your God is with you wherever you go.

— Joshua 1:9

A Cowgirl Prayer

Dear Heavenly Father,
You did not create this Cowgirl Spirit just for cowgirls.
You bestowed this spirit upon the cowgirls of the past
to show me how I, too, can become just like them—
conquering with trust, loving without worry,
keeping laughter and joy in my heart, and living
my life fearlessly to achieve possibilities beyond my
comprehension.

Amen

About the Author

Jan Pflaum is a dairy farm girl from Indiana, who now lives in Texas. She has a nursing background and had worked in Hospice for many years. Hospice was an experience that forever changed her life. It was such a privilege for her to help those patients and their families during a very challenging part of their lives. Because of this experience she designed tee shirts and hats with the slogan, "Don't Allow Cancer to Dull Your Sparkle". This design is copywritten and in the archives in Washington, DC.

After moving to Texas and becoming intrigued by the Cowgirl spirit, Jan wanted to continue to design. She created the design, Cowgirl Up, Roping a Cure for Cancer, and an Inspirational video, which was filmed at the National Cowgirl Museum in Ft. Worth, Texas.

Jan quickly learned that the Cowgirl mindset is absolute — it resides within them, and manifests itself as an attitude and in the special way they live their lives.

She felt that everyone should have this great attitude, so she wrote the book Roping the Storms of Life Like a Cowgirl. The book and worksheets after each chapter show how others can achieve this mentality and soar above the exhausting trail they're riding at this very moment.

Jan says, "Cowgirls don't mess around. They don't back down from anything or anyone. They have the power and I think everyone can attain that same mindset, by Roping the Storms of YOUR life like a Cowgirl.

www.ingramcontent.com/pod-product-compliance
Lightning Source LLC
Chambersburg PA
CBHW050045080526
44586CB00014B/1458